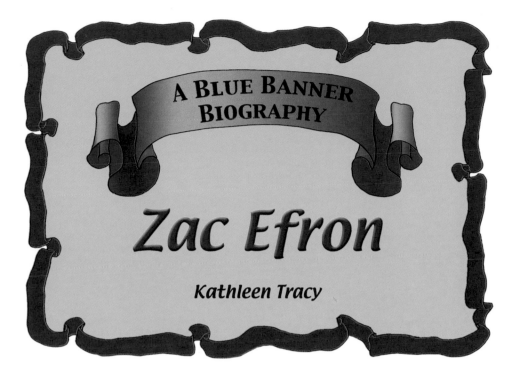

A BLUE BANNER
BIOGRAPHY

Zac Efron

Kathleen Tracy

Mitchell Lane
PUBLISHERS

P.O. Box 196
Hockessin, Delaware 19707
Visit us on the web: www.mitchelllane.com
Comments? email us: mitchelllane@mitchelllane.com

Mitchell Lane PUBLISHERS

Printing	2	3	4	5	6	7	8	9

Blue Banner Biographies

Akon	Alan Jackson	Alicia Keys
Allen Iverson	Ashanti	Ashlee Simpson
Ashton Kutcher	Avril Lavigne	Bernie Mac
Beyoncé	Bow Wow	Britney Spears
Carrie Underwood	Chris Brown	Chris Daughtry
Christina Aguilera	Christopher Paul Curtis	Ciara
Clay Aiken	Condoleezza Rice	Daniel Radcliffe
David Ortiz	Derek Jeter	Eminem
Eve	Fergie (Stacy Ferguson)	50 Cent
Gwen Stefani	Ice Cube	Jamie Foxx
Ja Rule	Jay-Z	Jennifer Lopez
Jessica Simpson	J. K. Rowling	Johnny Depp
JoJo	Justin Berfield	Justin Timberlake
Kate Hudson	Keith Urban	Kelly Clarkson
Kenny Chesney	Lance Armstrong	Lindsay Lohan
Mariah Carey	Mario	Mary J. Blige
Mary-Kate and Ashley Olsen	Michael Jackson	Miguel Tejada
Missy Elliott	Nancy Pelosi	Nelly
Orlando Bloom	P. Diddy	Paris Hilton
Peyton Manning	Queen Latifah	Ron Howard
Rudy Giuliani	Sally Field	Selena
Shakira	Shirley Temple	Tim McGraw
Usher	**Zac Efron**	

Library of Congress Cataloging-in-Publication Data
Tracy, Kathleen.
  Zac Efron / by Kathleen Tracy.
    p. cm. — (Blue banner biographies)
  Includes bibliographical references and index.
  ISBN 978-1-58415-618-5 (library bound)
  1. Efron, Zac—Juvenile literature. 2. Actors—United States—Biography—Juvenile literature. I. Title.
PN2287.E395T73 2008
792.02'8092—dc22
[B]   2007019686

ABOUT THE AUTHOR: Kathleen Tracy has been a journalist for over twenty years. Her writing has been featured in magazines including *The Toronto Star's Star Week, A&E Biography* magazine, *KidScreen* and *Variety.* She is also the author of numerous biographies and other nonfiction books, including *Mariano Guadalupe Vallejo, William Hewlett: Pioneer of the Computer Age, The Watergate Scandal, The Life and Times of Cicero, Mariah Carey, Kelly Clarkson,* and *The Plymouth Colony: The Pilgrims Settle in New England* for Mitchell Lane Publishers. She divides her time between homes in Studio City and Palm Springs, California.

PHOTO CREDITS: Cover, p. 4 — Nina Prommer/Globe Photos; p. 7 — Michail Germana/Globe Photos; p. 12, 24 — Jeffrey Mayer/WireImage; p. 14 — John Barrett/Globe Photos; p. 18 — Patrick Riviere/Getty Images; p. 20 — Frazer Harrison/Getty Images; p. 22 — *High School Musical*; p. 26 — Jeff Vespa/WireImage

CONTENTS

Thanks to the success of High School Musical, *Zac Efron landed a role in the film adaptation of the Broadway musical* Hairspray. *The movie costars John Travolta, Michelle Pfeiffer, James Marsden, and Queen Latifah.*

Let's Put On a Show!

Zac Efron felt as if he were on the best kind of carnival ride. The previous six weeks had been a head-spinning whirlwind of performing and recording and traveling. He'd been so busy—and having so much fun—he hadn't had time to really think about what it all meant. All he knew was that *High School Musical* was like no other acting job he'd ever had.

It all began with an especially grueling audition. Usually the actor goes in, reads a scene or two from the script, maybe chats with the director and producers a little bit, then goes home. The process takes a half hour at the most. However, Zac's final audition for *High School Musical* lasted almost eight hours!

Over 600 young actors originally showed up hoping to be cast as one of the six leads. Eventually, the field had been narrowed down to 15 actors competing for each role. The final audition would determine who made it and who would be sent home disappointed. When Zac showed up, he was paired with another hopeful, Vanessa Hudgens. They were both nervous, but Zac says he and Vanessa felt comfortable with each other right away.

"Somehow the casting directors knew. Immediately we started having fun. We knew that we had a slim shot from the very beginning. We went in and gave it all we could."

> Zac was grateful for his theater experience . . . . The audition was "Broadway style—seven and a half hours of dancing, singing, and acting."

As the casting agents put the actors through their paces for a group of Disney executives and the filmmakers, Zac was grateful for his theater experience. "I had it easier than some guys—some of them were passing out!" he told *Scholastic News*. The audition was "Broadway style—seven and a half hours of dancing, singing, and acting."

Then, because his character was a star athlete, Zac also had to go play basketball. "I was probably weakest at that," he admits, "but I passed."

As the day wore on, the number of actors dwindled as the movie's director narrowed the finalists down to a handful. "They would tap people on the shoulder and send them home, saying they were no longer needed," Efron recalled in the *San Luis Obispo Tribune*.

Zac and Vanessa didn't get tapped. "At the end of the day our headshots were still together and we were still performing," Zac says.

At the 2006 Teen Choice Awards, held at Universal Studios in Los Angeles, Zac Efron won the Breakout Star award and High School Musical won for best Comedy/Musical Show. From left to right: Lucas Grabeel, Monique Coleman, Corbin Bleu, Ashley Tisdale, Zac Efron, and Vanessa Hudgens.

A week and a half later, Zac got the call—he'd been cast in the lead role, and Vanessa was his costar. "They picked us from the beginning," he says.

Efron and the others were whisked off to Utah, where they were put through a kind of performing boot camp for two weeks. "The training schedule was pretty intense," Zac said on MovieWeb.com. "We'd wake up every day for two weeks and . . . start practice at nine. That would be full dance practice, singing and everything.

"After that, I would go straight to basketball practice. We had to . . . get in the layup lines and run drills. At the end of the day I just remember being so beat and beyond tired. I reached a new level of sleep every night, it was crazy."

He admitted learning the choreography was the most difficult thing for him, and ended up with shin splints and sprained ankles. "By the end I'd sustained so many injuries and was so sore but so much better than I was before," he observed to *Scholastic News.* "I learned more in those two weeks than I'd learned in the previous years. Every second of it was worth it."

> **"I made a lot of good friends, and we see each other all the time. If I could go back and do it again I'd do it in a heartbeat."**

Immediately after the two-week rehearsal was over, filming began on location at East High School in Salt Lake City. As Zac told *Time for Kids,* the actors had all become good friends by then, so "It was a blast. The whole cast would hang out after every day of shooting. We'd go out and eat dinner and we just did fun stuff together and it made being on the set a lot more fun."

He later told *Scholastic News* that when filming was over, "Everyone was devastated. It was so hard not to be able to go to the hotel room next door and knock. I made a lot of good friends, and we see each other all the time. If I could go back and do it again I'd do it in a heartbeat."

That wish, and many more, was about to come true.

Stage Lights

Some actors know from the time they can first put a sentence together that they were born to perform. Others stumble into it. Johnny Depp, for example, was a twenty-two-year-old struggling musician when he went on his first audition—only because it sounded more fun than working as a telemarketer selling ballpoint pens. Then there are those who get nudged into it by a persistent parent.

Zachary David Alexander Efron was born on October 18, 1987, in San Luis Obispo, California. Located two and a half hours north of Los Angeles, the community began as a Spanish mission settlement but is now most famous for being home to the Hearst Castle.

Zac's dad, David, an electrical engineer, and his mom, Starla Baskett, raised Zac and his younger brother, Dylan, in the nearby town of Arroyo Grande. Zac grew up as a self-described comic book geek and an avid sports fan—the Los Angeles Lakers and the San Francisco Giants are his favorite teams. But as a young kid, Zac wasn't very athletic.

"I was too small," he told PBSKids.org. "It took me a long time before I actually started growing. I was bad at Little League baseball and I think I scored two points my entire basketball season."

He admitted in a *Newsweek* online chat, "I was the worst kid on my sixth-grade basketball team. I passed the ball to the wrong team and they scored at the buzzer in double overtime to win the championship. It's one of those memories that still makes you squirm when you think about it."

"It's one of those memories that still makes you squirm when you think about it."

Zac may not have been destined for basketball stardom, but he was a good singer. When he was eleven, his dad urged him—strongly—to audition for an upcoming production of the musical *Gypsy* at the nearby Pacific Conservatory of the Performing Arts.

"Yeah, I was actually forced by my dad into my first musical," he revealed to *It's My Life.* "My dad convinced me to go out and audition. I said yes, thinking it was a few months away and I'd somehow talk myself out of it by then. Little did I know it was like the next day! So I went into this audition kicking and screaming."

Once he got the part, Zac realized that his dad "had just showed me the coolest thing on earth. He opened so many doors for me. I started auditioning for every single play that

Zac's eighth-grade drama teacher believed her student had the talent to be a professional actor. He took her advice to heart and began driving to Los Angeles several times a week to go on TV series and film auditions.

was in our area. Luckily, I booked some of the roles and started doing very well."

Other stage roles followed, including parts in *The Music Man, Mame, Little Shop of Horrors,* and *Peter Pan,* in which he played John. "That was a really fun part because I got to fly around on a fly wire," he told the *Columbus Dispatch.* "I was hovering over people in the audience. I actually knocked off a guy's toupee once."

Zac was hooked. "From day one, I got addicted to being onstage and getting the applause and laughter," he said in the *San Luis Obispo Tribune.* Even so, he told *Scholastic News,* "There was never really a point where I sat down and said I wanted to be an actor. It was a culmination of events that led me here."

> "When you get made fun of, when people point out your weaknesses, that's just another opportunity for you to rise above."

He went to acting classes and took singing lessons, learned to play the piano and read music — and became the butt of bullies for it in middle school.

"Constantly," he admitted on PBSKids.org. "That's what built my character. That's what makes you who you are. When you get made fun of, when people point out your weaknesses, that's just another opportunity for you to rise above."

How?

"You laugh with it. If someone calls you names and you laugh they have no grounds to make fun of you for it ever again."

Although Zac was having a great time doing stage musicals, his eighth-grade drama teacher believed he had the talent to go much farther than local productions. She told Zac he should start auditioning for television and movie roles. His parents agreed.

Now the question was, would Hollywood agree, too?

Hollywood Calls

No kid actor can succeed professionally without the support of parents who often make great sacrifices on behalf of their child. In Zac's case, that was a mom willing to drive from San Luis Obispo to Los Angeles—five hours round trip—three times a week so that he could go on auditions. Luckily, it wasn't long before the effort began to pay off.

Zac's first TV role was in *Firefly*, the 2002 sci-fi adventure series from *Buffy the Vampire Slayer* creator Joss Whedon. Over the next couple of years, several other small parts followed, including a part on *ER*. As he told *San Luis Obispo Tribune* reporter Patrick Pemberton, it wasn't as easy as it may have looked.

"For every role that I have done on TV and movies, I've auditioned for thirty or forty," Zac said. Sometimes he had as many as ten callbacks, only to see someone else get the role in the end. "It's ruthless. There are several thousand kids out there with brown hair and blue eyes

Zac and his Derby Stallion *costar, Crystal Hunt. Zac's outgoing personality helps him make friends easily, both on the set and off.*

that are my age trying to be in movies. Getting a job is like beating a casino."

If that was true, then Efron was about to hit a jackpot.

His first important break finally came in 2004 when he was cast as an autistic teenager in the TV movie *Miracle Run*. Thomas Lewis costarred as his brother.

To prepare, Zac says he "read a book on autism called *Thinking in Pictures*. It is about how the world looks through [an autistic person's] eyes. . . . You've got to look at a situation from their perspective."

Although the movie came and went without much notice, Zac was singled out. A review in *Daily Variety* noted, "Efron and Lewis are commendable in their performances for not resorting to stereotypes of the developmentally disabled. Each gets their moment to shine with a savant talent, giving the story the foundation it needs to wrap up with an optimistic finish."

Even though his acting career was taking up more and more of his time, Zac was still a straight-A student at San Luis Obispo High. He once admitted he'd get upset with himself if he got even one B on his report card.

"My priority had always been school first, acting second," he told *Scholastic News*. "Then acting took off and school got put a bit on the back burner—but not too much. I have a really high grade point average. But if I hadn't taken the acting route I think I might have been valedictorian." He also reported, "I've applied to USC and UCLA."

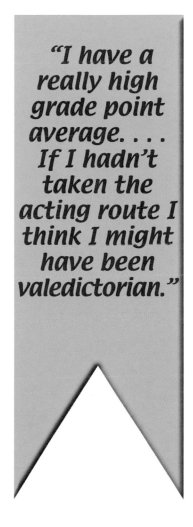

"I have a really high grade point average. . . . If I hadn't taken the acting route I think I might have been valedictorian."

Although he enjoyed high school, Efron admitted in a MovieWeb.com interview that it wasn't always easy being the guy who acts. "All my extracurricular activities were involved with performing, singing and dancing, and theater; reactions were mixed. . . . To go out and be in plays at the local theater houses wasn't that cool I guess. So that was one of the things I had to overcome—peer pressure against theater. I just tried to follow what I really wanted to do."

Being unwilling to conform to others' expectations made Zac more accepting of other students. "I really didn't have a clique. I was more of a floater, I tried to hang out with everyone, I had friends in all the groups."

Since he didn't participate in his school's drama department, Zac always invited his friends to his stage performances.

"It would be really fun to have your friends come and watch the shows because then they could see what the heck you're doing all this time when you're missing school and aren't able to hang out."

> *Since he didn't participate in his school's drama department, Zac always invited his friends to his stage performances.*

His friends would be seeing even less of Zac when a guest spot on the WB television series *Summerland* earned him a spot as a full-time cast member during its second season. Efron described his character, Cameron Bale, as "your basic kid-next-door type of guy. Only . . . he's going to get pretty twisted."

Zac told KidzWorld.com that not long after filming started, he shot his first on-screen kiss with costar Kay Panabaker. "Those are really tough, but everyone made me feel right at home. It was a blast because we got it out of the way. It made me feel like a part of the cast."

While on the series, Zac finished an independent study program that included college courses and online classes. He graduated from high school six months early and was accepted at USC, where he planned to attend film school. However, a little movie called *High School Musical* would put those plans on hold.

CHAPTER
4

The Phenomenon

*T*he interesting thing about acting is that you never know
what a role is going to demand. For *The Derby Stallion,* Zac
learned how to ride a horse.

Young Star News reported that it was Efron's first time
in the saddle. "I assumed when I signed on for this movie
that it was all going to be done by stuntmen," Zac admitted.
"Then the first day when I came on the set and talked to one
of our producers, he said, 'You have three lessons and
you're going to be jumping!' "

Zac said that until then, "Horses were never something
I thought I'd be interested in. But the first time I got on the
horse I realized I was completely wrong. . . . It's *fun!* It's
so thrilling."

And so painful. Learning how to ride used muscles
Efron never knew he had. "Oh, *man,*" he groaned, "it was
some of the worst pains I ever had in my entire life!"

It was almost as bad as the beating he took rehearsing
for *High School Musical.* However, Zac said the sprains and

High School Musical *was a worldwide phenomenon. To promote the movie, Zac and his costars traveled to Australia. They posed for pictures outside Sydney's Quay restaurant. From left to right: Vanessa Hudgens, Zac Efron, Monique Coleman, and Ashley Tisdale.*

aches were worth being able to combine his two loves—theater and film. He explained to *Time for Kids* reporter Emily Doveala that he wanted the movie to "bring musicals back into the spotlight," but, as he stressed on MovieWeb.com, "in a modern way. We used pop and rock and just some cool, funky grooves that kids could relate to."

Although all the actors had great fun making the movie and thought kids and teenagers would enjoy it, they were completely unprepared for the reaction it generated.

Zac admitted that during filming, "Everyone said how great it looked . . . but we're in the industry and we're used to hearing that. I was expecting the worst just for my own sanity. But after it aired . . . watching everyone's reaction was amazing."

Within a day of *High School Musical*'s premiere on January 20, 2006, over a half million people visited the movie's Web site. The sound track ended up being the biggest-selling CD in 2006. The single "Breaking Free" went platinum, meaning over one million copies were sold, and five other singles from the show were certified gold, having sold a half million each.

In July 2006, the Television Critics Association voted *High School Musical* the outstanding children's show of the

"Everyone said how great it looked. . . . But after it aired . . . watching everyone's reaction was amazing."

High School Musical *was one of the most honored TV programs of 2006. In July, the Television Critics Association voted it the outstanding children's show of the year. It also made a star out of Zac, who put off going to college to film the sequel.*

year. A month later, it earned six Emmy nominations and would go on to win two: for Outstanding Choreography and for Outstanding Children's Program. Zac won a Teen Choice Award for Breakout Star.

Local stage productions of the film appeared in schools and communities all across America, and it was just as big a hit in Europe and Australia. The cast, minus Zac (who was working on *Hairspray*), went on a sold-out, 42-date concert tour. *High School Musical* was a genuine phenomenon.

"The cast . . . was really focused and able to accomplish more than we should have been allowed to in [six weeks]."

The film's director was choreographer extraordinaire Kenny Ortega, best known for his work on the movie *Dirty Dancing*. He praised Zac and the other actors. "In the old days, it took six weeks just to film the dance number. Now you get six weeks to do the entire film," Ortega pointed out to writer Susan Young. "There was tremendous pressure. I've always said that *High School Musical* owes a lot to the cast, which was really focused and able to accomplish more than we should have been allowed to do in the time we were given."

What's most surprising to some people is that the story was a familiar one. In the movie, Zac plays outgoing basketball jock Troy Bolton. Gabriella (Vanessa Hudgens)

In High School Musical, *Troy Bolton (played by Zac Efron) and Gabriella Montez (Vanessa Hudgens) sing a duet. The movie would be nominated for six Emmys and would win two: for Outstanding Choreography and for Outstanding Children's Program.*

is a shy new student who enjoys math and science. When they become friends and decide to try out for the upcoming East High School musical together, they have to overcome the disapproval of their respective cliques and the resentment of the theater group.

"The message from the movie is that you have to be yourself," Efron explained to *Scholastic.* "There are always cliques in high school — walk your own path."

And that's just what Zac intended to keep doing.

A Bright Future

The tremendous success of *High School Musical* catapulted Zac into overnight stardom. His picture has adorned the cover of every teen magazine, and teen and tween girls around the world follow his every movement. Efron takes it all in good-natured stride.

"It's not too bad. I'm not getting mobbed or anything," he says, then jokes, "but I can't go out to places where there's going to be lots of people under fifteen."

Fortunately, he says, "I am lucky enough to have friends so far from the industry that they don't care. I come home and it's a reality check. It's a free coupon to deflate your head. It is great to go home and hang out. I'm the same kid. It is when you are in the industry with actors and actresses that maybe your perspective gets changed."

Sometimes, success changes your perspective for the better and prompts actors to use their celebrity to help others less fortunate. In May 2006, Efron attended the Fourth Annual Dennis Quaid Charity Weekend in Austin,

Zac calls rumors "the dirty side" of Hollywood success. He says he's comfortable with his success and credits his fans with being so supportive.

Texas, and played in the golf tournament hosted by Quaid. The weekend-long benefit raised over $300,000 for four local children's charities.

Zac has also learned to take all the media attention in stride—such as the reports that he and costar Ashley Tisdale were romantically linked. "Rumors are always gonna be a part of it—that's the dirty side," he acknowledged on PBSKids.org. "It comes with the territory."

So does typecasting. While Zac is grateful for everything that has happened to him since *High School Musical*, a couple of months after the sequel would air in August 2007, he would turn twenty. Efron knows it can be tricky for "kid stars" to make a successful transition to adult roles. His plan is to take it slow and bring his fans along for the ride.

"I would love to do edgier roles but it needs to be the right project with a good story . . . ," he said in a *Newsweek* chat. "In a few years, when I do more adult projects, my fans also will be a little more mature so it'll be fun to grow up with them."

He gets a chance to show off a more grown-up side in the feature film *Hairspray.* Another musical, the cast includes John Travolta, Michelle Pfeiffer, Queen Latifah, James Marsden, and Amanda Bynes.

"I would love to do edgier roles but it needs to be the right project with a good story."

Precisely because of Zac's clean-cut image, *Hairspray* director Adam Shankman admitted in *Newsweek* that he initially had doubts Zac was right for the part. His first impression of Efron was "very Disney, very Mouseketeery."

Shankman changed his mind after Zac's audition and now is an outspoken supporter. "He's a really special kid and is arguably the biggest teen star in America right now."

To play the part of 1960s-era heartthrob Link Larkin, Zac cut his hair short, dyed it a darker brown, and gained 15 pounds. In *High School Musical,* someone else had to sing his songs because Zac's voice was too deep. For *Hairspray,* he was able to sing all his own songs, and joked to writer Johnnie Roberts that the movie allowed him to "regain some of my vocal dignity."

For his role in Hairspray, *Zac gained fifteen pounds and dyed his hair. In the movie, Zac plays teen heartthrob Link Larkin and gets to show off his singing and dancing skills. Efron hopes that* High School Musical *and* Hairspray *help increase the popularity of movie musicals.*

Production for *Hairspray* began in summer of 2006 with two months of rehearsal before filming from September to December. "The rehearsal process for this movie was longer than it took to rehearse *and* film *High School Musical*," Zac notes. "It was crazy."

After a few weeks off, Efron began working on the *High School Musical* sequel in early 2007. His busy work schedule forced him to temporarily put off his college plans. "I deferred my first year of college. Thankfully I still have a spot at USC."

When asked if he has any advice for other teenagers, Zac urges everyone to "do something that scares you every day because it's the only way you can test how far you can really go. Whether it's auditioning for the play or trying out for the basketball team, you have to explore your boundaries and see where you really want to go."

If that turns out to be performing, Zac says to "get involved. Be a part of a school production—whether it's set decorating, acting or lighting. Start in your community and get as much experience as possible. Being an actor sounds glamorous but it's hard work and lots of rejection. You have to really love it to be in this business."

For Zac Efron, there's no place he'd rather be.

> "Do something that scares you every day because it's the only way you can test how far you can really go."

CHRONOLOGY

1987 Zac is born on October 18 in San Luis Obispo, California.

1999 At the age of eleven, Zac makes his stage debut in a local production of *Gypsy*.

2002 He makes his TV debut in *Firefly*.

2004 Zac stars in *Miracle Run*, a TV movie that airs on the Lifetime cable network. He also joins the cast of the TV series *Summerland*.

2005 Zac is nominated for a Young Artist Award for his performance in *Miracle Run*. He appears in the music video for Hope Partlow's "Sick Inside." He is chosen for the lead role of Troy Bolton in *High School Musical*.

2006 *High School Musical* debuts on January 20 on the Disney Channel. Zac is cast as Link Larkin in the film adaptation of the Broadway musical *Hairspray*. He wins a Teen Choice Award for Breakout Star.

2007 Zac begins work on *High School Musical 2: Sing It All or Nothing!*

FILMOGRAPHY

2007 *High School Musical 2: Sing It All or Nothing!* (TV)
Hairspray
2006 *The Replacements* (voice/TV episode)
Heist (guest spot/TV series)
The Suite Life of Zack and Cody (guest spot/TV series)
High School Musical (TV)
NCIS (guest spot/TV series)
If You Lived Here, You'd Be Home Now (TV)
2005 *The Derby Stallion*
CSI: Miami (guest spot/TV series)
2004 *Summerland* (TV series)
Miracle Run (TV)
The Guardian (guest spot/TV series)
Triple Play (TV)
2003 *ER* (guest spot/TV series)
The Big Wide World of Carl Laemke (TV)
2002 *Firefly* (guest spot/TV series)

DISCOGRAPHY

2007 *High School Musical 2: The Soundtrack*
Hairspray, Motion Picture Soundtrack
2006 *High School Musical: The Soundtrack*

FURTHER READING

Further Reading

Norwich, Grace. *Zac Attack: An Unauthorized Biography*. New York: Price Stern Sloan, 2006.

Works Consulted

Carr, Kevin. "A Look at 'High School Musical'" http://ofcs.rottentomatoes.com/click/movie-1160789/reviews.php?critic=interview&page=1&rid=1507429

Churnin, Nancy. "Learning to Be 'High School' Stars: Try Community Theater, Young Actors Advise." *Dallas Morning News*. June 1, 2006.

The Columbus Dispatch: " 'Musical' Star Likes Newfound Fame" http://www.dispatch.com/news/now/now.php?story=dispatch/2006/09/20/20060920-H4-02.html

Crimson Celluloid, Interview with Zac Efron. http://www.lethaldeath.com/Crimson/Archives/ResidentDVDvil/Archives/RD_Interview_ZacEfron.php

Doveala, Emily. *Kid Scoops*. "The Scoop on 'High School Musical.' " http://www.timeforkids.com/TFK/kidscoops/story/0,14989,1169108,00.html

Gustafson, Amy Carlson. "Teens and Tweens Make 'High School' a Runaway Hit." http://www.keepmedia.com/pubs/PioneerPress/2006/02/02/1180996

KidzWorld: *Entertainment: Celebrity Vault.* "Zac Efron Biography." http://www.kidzworld.com/article/6784-zac-efron-biography

MovieWeb: *DVD News.* "Exclusive Interview: Zac Efron and Vanessa Anne Hudgens Sing Their Praises for *High School Musical*" http://www.movieweb.com/dvd/news/56/12756.php

Newsweek: *Newsweek Business,* "Ashley and Zac Talk Back!" http://www.msnbc.msn.com/id/14015421/site/newsweek/

PBS Kids: *It's My Life.*"Celebs: Zac Efron." http://pbskids.org/itsmylife/celebs/interviews/zac.html

Pemberton, Patrick S. "He Acts, He Sings—and He's Local." http://www.keepmedia.com/pubs/SanLuisObispoTribune/2006/03/10/1275374

Roberts, Johnnie. "Disney's Star Machine." *Newsweek.* July 24, 2006. p. 42.

Young, Susan. "Bay Area Native Kenny Ortega Sees Emmy Gold for 'High School Musical' Musical Man." *Alameda Times-Star.* August 24, 2006.

On the Internet

Disney Channel: High School Musical
http://psc.disney.go.com/disneychannel/originalmovies/highschoolmusical/

Hairspray
www.hairspraymovie.com

Zac Efron Fan
http://www.zac-efron.us/

INDEX